BIBLICAL

DISCIPLINE

THAT MAKES

CHILDREN FUN!

William & Judy Farley

"FOR THE LORD DISCIPLINES THE ONE HE LOVES,
AND CHASTISES EVERY SON WHOM HE RECEIVES"
(HEBREWS 12:6)

CONTENTS

William & Judy Farley
Visit my website at https://www.amazon.com/William-P.-Farley/e/B001KHEYPO/ref=ntt_dp_epwbk_0

Printed in the United States of America

First Printing: Dec 2017
Pinnacle Communications

Preface

As my wife and I have traveled around the country doing parenting conferences, we occasionally encounter resistance to the biblical commands about disciplining children. This resistance has motivated us to present a more exhaustive study on discipline than that found in *Gospel Powered Parenting.*

In these pages you will discover the presuppositions that are the necessary building blocks for biblical discipline, some suggestions for the mechanics of child discipline, and some answers to the many objections that hamper biblical discipline.

May these pages produce eternal fruit in your children, grandchildren, and great grandchildren. May they enhance spiritual joy in your family, and happy parenting for the glory of God.

A Tale of Two Children

Anew family visited our church potluck. Their eight-year-old daughter, Cassie, was playing with the other children. When dinner was over, and it was time to go, her father turned to her. "Cassie, please get your coat. We're leaving in a few minutes." Although it was clear that Cassie heard her father, she ignored him, turned and went in the opposite direction.

Her father did nothing.

A few minutes passed. "Cassie," he said a bit louder. "Please get your coat. We are leaving." Again, Cassie gave no indication that she had heard her father or had any intent to obey. Instead, she began playing with the other children.

Now, speaking in a louder irritated voice, he said a third time, "Cassie, did you hear me? I said, please get your coat. We are leaving." Cassie gave her father a look that said, "Who do you think you are?" and turned back to the children she was playing with.

An anxious silence settled over our table as each parent waited to see who would win, Cassie or her now embarrassed father?

"Cassie, did you hear me?" (He was now yelling). "Get your coat. Why are you embarrassing me in front of my friends? You will be grounded for the rest of the day if you don't obey." Cassie finally found her coat and returned. She and her parents slid out the door in silence.

What had we witnessed? We had witnessed the fruit of Cassie's training. Her parents had *trained* her to ignore them until they yelled and threatened.

A few weeks later I was with another family and their nine-year-old, John. I had watched his parents work with him for several years. He had been an unusually strong-willed child. There had been tears, conflicts, temper tantrums, and attempts to manipulate his parents. But John's efforts had been in vain. Instead, John's parents had trained him to cheerfully obey on the first command.

We were on the side of a hill from which a spring flowed that joined a river in the valley below. John and his brothers were catching bugs and damming the spring. They were in boy heaven. John was trying to catch minnows in a small pool about 200 feet away. His father cupped his hands and shouted, "John, it's time to go."

John looked up and caught his father's eye. I remembered the battles. I remembered all the hours of discipline and affection. How would he respond? To my surprise, John immediately dropped his sticks and twigs, grabbed his hooded sweatshirt, and cheerfully ran to his father. No fighting. No whining. No arguing. No protesting. No pouting. No multiple requests. Just cheerful obedience on the first command.

Which child would you like to parent—Cassie or John? The answer is obvious. Everyone wants a child like John. But how to get that child is the question?

This pamphlet will show you how to train children that obey like John, children that you enjoy being with, children that make parenting a joy. Not only you, but their teacher, your relatives, and your adult friends will also enjoy them.

The Goal

What is the goal of parenting? If you are a Christian, the first goal is their salvation. You want them to be with you in heaven. The really big goal, however, the one parents don't often think about, is the glory of God. Because your children glorified him, on the last day you want to hear God say, "Well done good and faithful servant." But that won't happen without discipline and training. "A child who does not respect the authority of his parents," writes Tim Challies, "will never respect the authority of his Creator. If we fail to discipline our children to obey us, we fail to discipline them to submit to God."

There is another goal, and ultimately it is less important, but it is a big motivator for most. You also want to *enjoy* your children, you want to *like* them, you want children that honor your authority, and make life easy for you. God wants that also, and he has given you the key—biblical discipline. Ultimately, those who spoil their children will not enjoy their company. But those who diligently discipline and train their children will enjoy being with them.

The Bible tells us that well-disciplined children make parents happy.[1] "Discipline your son, and he will give you rest; he will give *delight* to your heart" (Proverbs 29:17). By contrast, undisciplined children shame their parents. "A child left to himself brings *shame* to his mother" (Proverbs 29:15). Delight or shame? Those are the options. John was a delight, but Cassie shamed her parents.

The Bible provides little instruction on parenting. Only two New Testament verses address it, and they are similar. "Fathers, do not provoke your children to anger, but bring them up in the *discipline* and instruction of the Lord" (Ephesians 6:4). "Fathers, do not provoke your children, lest they become discouraged" (Colossians 3:21). Therefore, most of the Biblical instruction on parenting is in the Old Testament, specifically Proverbs. In fact, Paul wrote

---

[1] See Proverbs 17:6, and 23:24

Ephesians 6:4 with Proverbs in mind, so in a moment we will turn to Proverbs to define what the "discipline of the Lord" looks like. But before we do that we need to take a few pages to discuss some crucial presuppositions. They are the building blocks for effective parenting.

The Presuppositions of Biblical Discipline

Every new parent comes to the task of parenting ill-prepared. Since he or she has never parented before, without compelling outside influence, we will just imitate our parents. Our parents example may be biblical. It may be sub-biblical. It may be unbiblical. So, before we imitate our parents, let's re-think discipline through a biblical framework.

Like a wood-workers lathe, our presuppositions shape our parenting. If we are Christians, we are supposed to get our presuppositions from the Bible. But that is not always the case. The problem with presuppositions is that we get them from a variety of places—the Bible, parents, movies, school, television, general culture—and, we are generally unconscious of where we got them. Therefore we seldom discuss them or think about them. They are just assumed. So let's compare our presuppositions about parenting to the biblical presuppositions that produce children like John.

Transferring the Baton

Our first presupposition is that parenting is the process of passing the baton to our children[2]. In a 400-meter relay, the baton gets passed each hundred meters. The team that wins the race is usually the team that passes the baton most efficiently, without breaking stride.

---

[2] For more on this, see my book, *Gospel Powered Parenting.*

The baton being transferred is our self-control and values. We want our children to love what we love and disapprove of all that we disapprove of. We also want our children to be self-controlled, disciplined, able to persevere through obstacles. Without self-control, no one can achieve or have healthy relationships. We also want them to love God, to be humble, meek, unselfish, and hardworking.

Generally, from birth parents only have a six to eight-year window to pass this baton. After that it becomes increasingly difficult. The longer we wait to begin the discipline process the more unlikely the baton will ever get transferred.

Always Training

Our second assumption is that we are always training. Michael Thonet (d. 1871) was a French furniture designer. He developed what is now called, bentwood furniture. He discovered that beachwood rods, saturated in hot steam, could be bent into just about any shape. When the wood cooled it would hold that shape indefinitely. One of his models, chair number 14, has sold over fifty million copies.

Training a child is similar. It is the process of shaping your child's will and desires into something that resembles God's holiness. The hot pressure is your discipline and affection. When applied consistently over a significant period, your child's character will begin to resemble God's moral beauty, and when the heat is removed your child's moral character will retain that shape.

The crucial point is that the *shaping is never not happening*. You are always bending your child in one direction or another. He or she will take whatever shape you demand and reinforce. Cassie's parents had shaped her into what she was. They did not insist on obedience until, after multiple commands, they threatened with a raised voice. They had trained her to ignore them and she had responded. She had assumed the shape they had trained her to assume.

We are always training!

By contrast, John's parents taught him from an early age that he was expected to obey when the first command was uttered with a gentle voice. Here is how they applied the steam. After he learned to walk they asked him to come to them. Like most children, he looked at them and went the other way, so they picked him up, spanked him, waited until he finished crying, hugged and forgave him, put him back, and started over. "John, please come to your mother." They repeated this process until he came on the first command.

What were they doing? They were training. They were applying the steam of discipline to his fallen will. They were bending and shaping him to obey their commands. They were training him to respond on the *first* command.

Why were they doing this? They were doing it for God's sake. They wanted John to glorify him, and John would only do this to the degree that he was trained to obey. They were also doing it for their sake. They wanted to enjoy John. And, they were doing it for John, knowing that scripture promises that it will go well with children who honor their parents (Exodus 20:6). They knew this would only happen to the degree that he was taught to obey on the first command.

In the same way, Cassie was merely doing what her parents had trained her to do. Their expectations were sub-biblical, and they reaped what they expected.

God Is the Model

Our third presupposition is obvious. God is the model parent. Christian parents are duty bound to imitate him. He not only sets the bar, he is the bar, and God is a disciplinarian. He disciplines the sons that he loves.

> "And have you forgotten the exhortation that addresses
> you as sons? "My son, do not regard lightly the discipline

of the Lord, nor be weary when reproved by him. For the Lord *disciplines* the one he loves, and chastises every son whom he receives." It is for *discipline* that you have to endure.

God is treating you as sons. For what son is there whom his father does not *discipline*? If you are left without discipline, in which all have participated, then you are illegitimate children and not sons. Besides this, we have had earthly fathers who *disciplined* us and we respected them. Shall we not much more be subject to the Father of spirits and live? For they *disciplined* us for a short time as it seemed best to them, but he *disciplines* us for our good, that we may share his holiness.

For the moment, all discipline seems painful rather than pleasant, but later it yields the peaceful fruit of righteousness to those who have been trained by it" (Hebrews 12:5–11).

This passage teaches several lessons. First, God is holy. Holy people, like God, are happy, and therefore his goal is our holiness. God disciplines us that we might share his holiness. Holiness is a constellation of heart attitudes such as humility, gratitude, unselfishness, love, mercy, justice, perseverance, self-control, respect for authority, etc. Therefore, holiness of heart should also be the objective of our discipline.

Second, Hebrews twelve teaches that love *motivates* God's discipline. In fact, being disciplined is a sign that we are loved by God, that we are members of his family. This means that affection, not anger, motivates God's discipline. God always "disciplines for our good." He always has our best interest in mind.

Third, we learn that "for the moment all discipline seems painful rather than pleasant." That means our heavenly Father is no sentimental push over. He is willing to make it hurt. To be effective we also must be willing to make our discipline hurt.

Indwelling Sin

Our fourth presupposition is that your child has a problem. It is not what they do. It is their nature. What they do is a fruit of their nature. The baby conceived in each mother's womb is sinful. That means the problem is who your child is. Their behavior is secondary. Your child is *by nature* self-centered, proud, unbelieving, ungrateful, self-willed, and rebellious. They are this way from the moment of conception. "Folly is bound up in the heart of a child" (Proverbs 22:15).

This means your child is not basically good, as secular culture teaches. Instead, "We were by nature children of wrath" (Ephesians 2:3). If your child's nature was essentially good, you would need to teach them to be selfish, to throw temper tantrums, and to be ungrateful. These would not be natural. But, you don't need to teach these: they come automatically. The first words most children learn are not, "mommy, how can I serve you?" They're "no," or "mine!" This means you need to train your child to be godly. It will not come naturally.

Shaping Is Difficult

Our fifth presupposition is simple. In most cases the process of shaping your child's character will not be easy. Some children come out of the womb relatively compliant. For these the shaping process is short and less stressful. Others come out of the womb, as James Dobson says, smoking cigars and giving orders.[3] Shaping this child's character will be a struggle, a contest of wills—who is going to win, you or the child that God has sovereignly put in your care?

---

[3] See James Dobson, *The Strong Willed Child*

Remember, your son or daughter belongs to God. You are merely a steward. Therefore, it is imperative that you please God, not your child. To do this you must conquer your child's will. In some cases this will be all out war that lasts for four or five years.

Ashley came to me in tears. Her five-year-old would not obey. She was in a battle. She would spank him, and he would just immediately disobey again. No amount of pain was sufficient to deter him. She was getting angry, and she was afraid she would hurt him. I knew she and her husband well. They were excellent parents. "Don't give up," I exhorted her. "Persevere! He will change by age six or seven. Things will get better. He will start to obey. You are applying the steam, but he has not yet assumed the shape you desire."

She persevered. She didn't give up, and it paid off. He is now a model young adult, much like John.

Effective disciplinarians persevere in faith. What perseverance looks like will depend upon the child. I have five children. Two required very few spankings. In their case the wood was bent by age five. Another, however, required several spanking each day until he was about age seven. It was worth it. He is now the father of five well-behaved sons and the lead pastor of a growing church.

Dad Is the Chief Parent

Our last presupposition is that dad is the chief parent. Most reading this are probably mothers. That is because you carry the primary parenting load in the pre-adolescent years. But it is important to remember that, in the Bible, the fathers are the chief parents. The Bible addresses almost every command about parenting to fathers.

How do we apply this in the modern world? Fathers apply this when they are willing to assume responsibility for the parenting process. Fathers, communicate with your wife regularly. Talk about your children and their successes and failures. Recognize that on the day of final judgment God will hold you, not your wife, accountable for the parenting process.

The second application is for mothers. Communicate with your husband regularly. Settle upon a discipline policy. Carry it out. It is crucial that dad and mom are on the same page.

What if you are a single mom? God repeatedly promises to be a father to the fatherless. Read these verses. They will greatly encourage you. (Deuteronomy 10:18, 24:17, 27:19, Psalm 10:14, 68:5, 146:9, Isaiah 1:17, Jeremiah 22:3, Malachi 3:5). God has a special place of compassion and mercy for the single mother raising her children solo.

William P. Farley

The Mechanics of Biblical Discipline

What would effective child discipline look like? The Bible does not give us specifics, so what follows is just a suggestion. Don't make it into a law or rule. How we structure the discipline *event* will depend upon the specific goals that we have in mind. What do we want our discipline to accomplish? We mentioned some long-term goals earlier. Here are more. They are the *immediate* goals of the discipline event.

First, Christian parents want the discipline event to preach the gospel to their children.

Second, Christian parents want to impress their children with the truth that holiness leads to happiness, and that sin always leads to pain. How much better for them to make that connection through the discipline of a loving parent than by one day learning it through a failed marriage, getting fired from a job, or while incarcerated.

Third, we want to convince the child that God's love and God's discipline are inseparable. Here is one suggested way to accomplish these goals.

I call it a "discipline event" because that is what it is—an event. Don't just start swinging at your child in the heat of anger. Instead, take the child aside privately, to a bedroom, bathroom, or some other place where you can be alone.

Next hold the child in your lap. (Physical touch communicates love, care, and concern). Labor to help your child see the seriousness of sin. The conversation might go like this. "When I didn't give you the piece of candy you wanted, you began to pout. But, pouting is sinful. It displeases God. Gratitude is the proper response. Pouting is so serious that, were it not for the gospel, your pouting would have grave ramifications. For grumbling God destroyed the nation of Israel. The cross of Christ makes one thing clear. You don't deserve candy. You don't *deserve* anything. Nevertheless, look at how God loves you. You have loving parents, three meals a day, and a warm bed to sleep in. In addition, your parents love you enough to discipline you and teach you the gospel.

Because I love you I am going to spank you. I want to convince you that pouting is deeply displeasing to God, that he judges it, and that it always ends in pain."

Next you need to spank the child hard enough to cause pain but without injury. This is very important. False compassion will not want to cause pain. Real compassion deliberately makes it painful. We do this because God's discipline is painful. Remember Hebrews 12:11? "For the moment, *all discipline seems painful rather than pleasant*, but later it yields the peaceful fruit of righteousness to those who have been trained by it."

Next rehearse the gospel with your child. They can never hear it enough. It might go something like this. "You will not come under God's condemnation for this sin. Why? Because Jesus went to the cross and took the punishment that you deserve." What are you doing? You are teaching your child the gospel. In your child's thinking you are building a bridge between God's discipline and God's love.

Once the child quits crying and calms down, move to reconciliation. This is very important. Have the child ask God's forgiveness. "God, please forgive me" is not enough. It is crucial that they name the specific sin. "God, please forgive me for *pouting*." Next, have them ask your forgiveness. If they have sinned against someone else in the family be sure that they get reconciled to that person as well.

Last, express your love and affection. "I am so proud of you for taking responsibility for your behavior, admitting that it is wrong, confessing it, and asking God's forgiveness. I love you. In fact, it is because I love you so much that I spank you. I am imitating God. He disciplines the children he loves."

In most cases, your child will leave the room with a cleansed conscience, aware of both your love and God's. It is not unusual for them to skip out the door, happy, contented, and forgiven.

What should you do if you have an eight-year-old that you have trained to be like Cassie, and this is all new? Start by asking his or her forgiveness. Explain that you have not obeyed God, that you have not loved them as God commands, and that from now on you are only going to ask once. Promise change: then follow through.

William P. Farley

Objections to Biblical Discipline

The great barrier to biblical discipline is parental sin, the first of which is laziness. While preparing dinner you ask Isaac to set the table. He ignores you. You are busy. Everything in you wants to nag, raise your voice, or threaten. But this is a mistake. Remember, you are training. You are training your child to obey on the first command. Good disciplinarians are not controlled by their feelings. Love for the child and a passion for God's glory controls them. So, you drop what you are doing, and take the child through the discipline process.

Another sin to be overcome is unbelief. In recent decades spanking has become controversial. However, it has been the normal form of child discipline since the beginning of civilization.

God's ways are not our ways. His ways are not the ways of our child-centered world either. Western Culture considers spanking "child abuse," a work of violence that trains children to eventually themselves become violent. But scripture teaches the opposite: failure to spank is child abuse. "Whoever spares the rod *hates* his son, but he who loves him is diligent to discipline him" (Proverbs 13:24).

In fact, spanking is God's plan to drive violence from your child's heart. "Blows that wound cleanse away *evil* [that includes violence]; strokes make clean the innermost parts." (Proverbs 20:30). Also consider, "Do not withhold discipline from a child; if you strike him with a rod, he will not die. If you strike him with the rod, you will save his soul from Sheol" (Proverbs 23:13–14).

Many object, "This seems awfully strong. Surely, the rod is just a metaphor for other forms of valid discipline." However, this objection is not honest with the clear meaning of scripture. Tremper Longman III (Ph.D. Yale University), the Robert H. Gundry Professor of Biblical Studies at Westmont College, has authored or coauthored more than twenty books, including a number of Old Testament commentaries. Referring to Pr. 23:13-14, he notes, "...but here we are looking at those passages that explicitly mention physical discipline. And this is most often signaled by the Hebrew word *sebet*, which we translate as 'rod'. The 'rod' is not to be taken metaphorically... but rather as a tool of physical discipline."[4]

Scripture reminds us that sin is a heart-issue, and that God has given us the rod of discipline to conquer it. "Folly is bound up in the heart of a child, but the rod of discipline drives it far from him" (Proverbs 22:15). As already noted, scripture does not see spanking as a form of child-abuse. Just the opposite! It sees *the failure* to use the rod of discipline as the real child abuse.

Who will you believe?

Last, effective disciplinarians must conquer the fear of man. Both my parents and my in-laws thought we spanked too much. They disapproved. Many times, we would take a child to a private place for a spanking with the knowledge that our parents were in the other room criticizing. However, when the spankings were no longer needed they were thrilled with the fruit. Our children respected and obeyed them. They were fun to be around. The contrast with their other grandchildren that weren't disciplined was obvious.

---

[4] Tremper Longman III, Proverbs, (Grand Rapids: Baker Academic, 2006) pg. 564

Closing Cautions

Spanking should always be age appropriate. When a child is old enough to listen to reasoning, spankings should decrease or end. What is that age? The Bible doesn't say, but spanking should probably end somewhere between ages 8-12.

Second, don't ever spank in a grocery store aisle, a sidewalk, or anywhere else in public. Why? It will humiliate the child. In addition, it might get you reported for child abuse. Promise the child a spanking when you get home, and then follow through in private.

Third, don't ever physically abuse your child. Abuse means bruises, cuts, hitting the child in the face or head, kicking, etc. God is never pleased or glorified by child abuse. Your spankings should cause superficial stinging only.

Finally, you will fail. You will be tempted to give up on the strong-willed child. Sometimes you will revert to nagging. At other times, you will act out of self-interest instead of your child's best interest. You will not practice discipline consistently or perfectly.

This means that you will need the gospel. You will get discouraged. Your failures will mean condemnation. For this reason Jesus died. We are sinners. We are fallen. We are imperfect. We are inconsistent parents. We need the grace of forgiveness, and God freely gives it through the gospel. There is an unending supply. So go there and drink deeply!

Here is the bottom line. You will love the finished product. Parents that practice biblical discipline will ultimately find themselves delighting in their children. Your children will also enjoy you, and their siblings. Your parents and your children's teachers may object to corporeal discipline, but they will love the fruit—hard working, respectful, happy, well-adjusted young adults that glorify God.

And most importantly, on that final day, you will hear these wonderful words, "Well done good and faithful servant." And that is the ultimate prize.

About the Authors

William (Bill) was converted to Christ while doing graduate studies at Gonzaga University in 1971. He worked for 25 years in the business world while actively participating as a lay elder in his church. He sold his business in 1999 to pursue full time ministry. In 2002 he became the senior pastor of *Grace Christian Fellowship*, a non-denominational Evangelical church, which he planted with several other families in Spokane, Washington. It is now one church with two campuses.

Bill's writing experience includes the following:

- *Outrageous Mercy* (Baker Books, 2004, republished by P&R 2009),

- *Gospel Powered Parenting* (P&R 2009),

- *Gospel Powered Humility* (P&R Sept 2011),

- *Hidden in the Gospel* (P&R Feb 2014), and the

- *Secret to Spiritual Joy* (Cruciform 2015).

- He has written for *Discipleship Journal, Enrichment Journal*, a national pastor's magazine; *Focus On The Family Magazine, Pulpit Helps, The Journal of Biblical Counseling, Reformation 21*, and the *Spokesman Review*.

- His article, *God's Highest Passion* won high honors in the EPA's biblical exposition category.

- He has been a featured guest on numerous radio talk shows.

Bill and his wife, Judy, wrote this pamphlet together. They are profoundly thankful for their five children and their children's spouses. All of them, by God's grace alone, are believers. Three are full time pastors. All are actively involved in evangelical local churches. Although the parenting years had a few bumps in the road, God sustained them as they wept at the foot of his cross. He will do the same for you. There are no magic formulas for parenting, but there is a powerful God who loves us and honors our attempts to parent when we humbly look to him, obey his word and say, "We're sorry" when we fail. To him be the glory!

Made in United States
Orlando, FL
09 July 2023

34868131R00020